AUNG SAN SUU KYI

By William Thomas

WORLD ALMANAC® LIBRARY

Please visit our web site at: www.worldalmanaclibrary.com
For a free color catalog describing World Almanac® Library's list
of high-quality books and multimedia programs, call 1-800-848-2928 (USA)
or 1-800-387-3178 (Canada). World Almanac® Library's fax: (414) 332-3567.

Library of Congress Cataloging-in-Publication Data

Thomas, William, 1947-
    Aung San Suu Kyi / by William Thomas.
       p. cm. — (Trailblazers of the modern world)
    Includes bibliographical references and index.
    ISBN 0-8368-5494-2 (lib. bdg.)
    ISBN 0-8368-5263-X (softcover)
    1. Aung San Suu Kyi. 2. Burma—Politics and government—1948- . 3. Political activists—
Burma—Biography. I. Title. II. Series.
    DS530.53.A85T47   2004
    959.105'3'092—dc22
    [B]   2004043381

First published in 2005 by
World Almanac® Library
330 West Olive Street, Suite 100
Milwaukee, WI 53212 USA

Copyright © 2005 by World Almanac® Library.

Project manager: Jonny Brown
Editor: Jim Mezzanotte
Design and page production: Scott M. Krall
Photo research: Diane Laska-Swanke
Indexer: Walter Kronenberg

Photo credits: © AP/Wide World Photos: cover, 37, 42; © Dave Benett/Getty Images: 32; © Bettmann/CORBIS:
12, 41; © Bohemian Nomad Picturemakers/CORBIS: 7; © Margaret Bourke-White/Time Life Pictures/Getty
Images: 14; © Manuel Ceneta/AFP/Getty Images: 36; © CORBIS SYGMA: 21, 24, 39 top; © David Cumming;
Eye Ubiquitous/CORBIS: 13; © Aubert Dominique/CORBIS SYGMA: 6, 31; © Jeremy Horner/CORBIS: 4;
© Hulton Archive/Getty Images: 8; © Hulton-Deutsch Collection/CORBIS: 10, 11, 15; © Keystone/Getty Images:
9, 18; © Saeed Khan/AFP/Getty Images: 40; Scott M. Krall/© World Almanac Library, 2005: 5; © Christophe
Loviny/CORBIS: 16, 27; © Mansell/Time Life Pictures/Getty Images: 34; © Francis Miller/Time Life Pictures/Getty
Images: 19; © Mathew Polak/CORBIS SYGMA: 22; © Joseph Sohm; ChromoSohm Inc./CORBIS: 20; © Mario
Tama/AFP/Getty Images: 39 bottom; © Sandro Tucci/Time Life Pictures/Getty Images: 26 both, 28, 30, 33, 35;
© Adam Woolfitt/CORBIS: 17

Printed in the United States of America

1 2 3 4 5 6 7 8 9 08 07 06 05 04

TABLE of CONTENTS

Words that appear in the glossary are printed in **boldface**
type the first time they occur in the text.

CHAPTER 1

A SYMBOL AND A VOICE

A quiet street in a Myanmar village

On the afternoon of April 5, 1989, there was tension in the air in Danubyu, a modest village in the Asian country of Myanmar. A new political party, the National League for Democracy, had been speaking out against Myanmar's military government, and some members of the party were campaigning in the village. The government didn't allow criticism of its actions, and the residents of Danubyu were nervous about what might happen.

ONE TARGET INSTEAD OF MANY

That afternoon, some members of the National League for Democracy were returning from a meeting. They walked quietly down the main road of the village. Just ahead of them, a jeep pulled up. A squad of armed soldiers jumped out and blocked the road, and the officer in charge issued an order to the soldiers to get ready to shoot.

As the soldiers took up firing positions, a small, dark-haired woman urged the others in the group to move to the side of the road and stop. She continued forward alone, walking directly toward the soldiers and their raised weapons.

The woman was Aung San Suu Kyi (pronounced ong-sahn-sue-chee), a leader in the National League for Democracy. She was forty-three years old, a wife and the mother of two teenage sons. As a child, she had been so afraid of the dark that she wouldn't enter a room unless a light was turned on first. Throughout her life, friends had described her as quiet and shy. What was she thinking as she walked toward those guns? She thought that if the soldiers were going to shoot, it would be better to give them just one target instead of many.

This remarkable woman did not die that day. Just before the command to fire, a higher-ranking officer ran up and ordered the soldiers to lower their rifles and leave. He was later punished, while the officer who nearly gave the order to shoot was promoted. Then and now, those who have dared to defy the government have faced considerable danger. Yet since that afternoon, Suu Kyi has continued to fight for the rights of her people, despite being subjected to threats, violence, and imprisonment.

DICTATORSHIP IN THE GOLDEN LAND

Myanmar is located in Southeast Asia. For centuries, it was called Burma. It was once known to travelers as the Golden Land for its natural riches, its spectacular temples, and its friendly people. The country has had a troubled history, however, especially in the second half of the twentieth century.

A ruthless military **dictatorship** has ruled the nation for more than forty years. This government changed the name of the country to Myanmar in 1989 (see sidebar on page 6). The government has outlawed political parties that have opposed it and has ignored the results of democratic elections. Burmese citizens often cannot travel freely within their own country and can be arrested simply for gathering in groups of more than five.

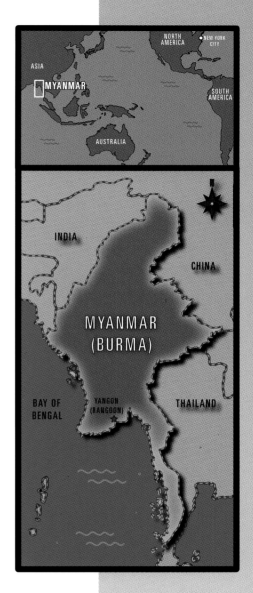

Countries bordering Myanmar include India, China, and Thailand.

AN INTERNATIONAL HERO

There have been many people in Myanmar who have spoken out against the dictatorship and have tried to bring a democratic government to the country. Some have died for their efforts, and others have been imprisoned and tortured.

Aung San Suu Kyi stands out among these courageous people. She is a symbol of resistance to the military government and the voice of Burmese citizens who hope for democracy. For her efforts to bring liberty and democracy to Myanmar, Suu Kyi has been honored by many international **human rights** organizations. Her speeches have been published in dozens of languages, and she has been the subject of books, magazine articles, and television programs around the world. She has received the Medal of Freedom from the U.S. government and the 1991 Nobel Peace Prize.

Daw Aung Suu Kyi in 1988

THE LADY

Despite all the honors she has received, Suu Kyi is a reluctant hero whose life is filled with contradictions. She never wanted a political career, yet she is the center of a political struggle. She passionately loves her homeland, but she has lived half her life in other countries. She is regarded as a

Police, soldiers, and spies observe the daily actions of people in Myanmar.

patriot by the Burmese people, but she is considered a traitor and a foreign agent by the government. Although she is devoted to nonviolence, she has witnessed murder, torture, and other forms of **oppression**. She is a champion of democracy and freedom, but the Burmese military government has taken away her own freedom through imprisonment.

There is another contradiction to the story of Suu Kyi. Although *Daw* ("Miss") Suu Kyi is the most famous person in Myanmar, her name is almost never written or spoken in her homeland. Her supporters fear punishment if they speak favorably of her, and her opponents in the military government don't want her name publicized. Everyone in Myanmar—both those who love and respect her, and those who hate and fear her—refer to Suu Kyi simply as "The Lady."

The Meaning of Daw

Daw is a Burmese word that means "aunt," but it is used in the way "Miss" and "Mrs." are used in English. It is a term of respect and affection. For men, the term used is *U* (rhymes with zoo), which means "uncle." U is also a common man's name.

In The Quiet Land

A poem by Aung San Suu Kyi

In the Quiet Land, no one can tell
If there's someone who's listening for secrets they can sell
The informers are paid in the blood of the land
And no one dares speak what the tyrants won't stand

In the Quiet Land of Burma, no one laughs and no one
   thinks out loud
In the Quiet Land of Burma, you can hear it in the silence
   of the crowd
In the Quiet Land, no one can say
When the soldiers are coming to carry them away

In the Quiet Land, no one can hear
What is silenced by murder and covered up with fear
But despite what is forced, freedom's a sound
That liars can't fake and no shouting can drown

CHAPTER 2

THE DAUGHTER OF A HERO

It could be said that Suu Kyi was born to take a leading role in her country's affairs. Her father, Aung San, is a great Burmese hero. His place in Burmese history is an important part of Suu Kyi's story.

Aung San in uniform during World War II

A YOUNG LEADER

When Suu Kyi's father Aung San was born in 1915, Burma was part of India, then a British colony, and it had been under British rule since the 1800s. Burma eventually became a separate British colony. In the 1930s, the young Aung San led a student movement that sought independence for Burma. Aung San was briefly jailed by British authorities for his activities with this movement.

In 1940, Aung San went to Japan, where he organized the Burma Independence Army (BIA). By then, World War II (1939–1945) had begun. In 1941, when Japanese troops invaded Burma, BIA troops were with them, led by Aung San. By 1942, the Japanese had taken control of Burma.

That year, Aung San came down with **malaria** and was hospitalized. A nurse named Khin Kyi cared for him. Aung San fell in love with Khin Kyi, and the couple married and soon started a family. By 1945, they had two sons and another baby on the way. But their personal lives took second place to the war.

British and U.S. forces were struggling to regain control of Burma in 1945. By then, Aung San had become disillusioned with Burma's Japanese rulers, and he led Burmese soldiers in a surprise attack that defeated the Japanese. Two months after this victory, on June 19, 1945, Aung San and Khin Kyi became parents of their third child, a girl. They named her Aung San Suu Kyi.

MOVING TOWARD INDEPENDENCE

British and Indian troops advance toward a Japanese position in Burma during World War II. U.S. troops also fought in Burma.

After World War II ended, the British reestablished a colonial government. They understood, however, that their colonial rule was coming to an end and that Burma was moving toward independence. Aung San was a hero and the most popular man in Burma, and he was the only person supported by both the Burmese army and Burma's many **ethnic** groups. He was appointed to a position in the postwar colonial government.

At the time, Suu Kyi was just one year old. Her brother Aung San U was four and her other brother Aung San Lin was three. The family moved into a home in a quiet area of Rangoon, Burma's capital city. Their house, however, was rarely quiet. In addition to the

U Aung San arrives at 10 Downing Street, the residence of the British prime minister, to discuss the independence of Burma.

three children, there was a constant stream of visitors by day and night. These visitors included politicians, members of many ethnic groups, leaders of labor unions, and military men. They all worked with Aung San as he put together a plan to gain independence.

Although Aung San wanted the British to leave his country, he was not anti-British. At Rangoon University, he had studied English literature and history, and he admired the British system of **parliamentary** government. Late in 1946, he traveled to London for a series of meetings with the British prime minister, Clement Attlee. Together, they worked out an agreement that would make Burma an independent nation within one year.

Aung San returned home as the leader of a **transitional** government. He traveled around the country giving speeches, listening to different groups, and organizing details of the new government. Whenever possible, his wife Daw Khin Kyi and their three children accompanied him on these trips. It seemed certain that Aung San would be the first prime minister of an independent Burma.

TRAGEDY AND TRIUMPH

Aung San never became prime minister. On July 19, 1947, while he was in a meeting with the other leaders of the transitional government, an army vehicle pulled up outside the building. A group of heavily armed men got out. They burst into the meeting, sprayed the room with bullets, and escaped. In the

After the Assassination

After Aung San was assassinated, U Nu, a member of the transitional government who survived the bullets that killed his companions, was chosen as prime minister. He was Burma's first—and last—democratically elected leader.

The man who planned Aung San's assassination was U Saw, Burma's prime minister at the beginning of World War II. He believed that he, not Aung San, should lead Burma. U Saw and the others involved in Aung San's murder were caught, tried, convicted, and executed.

U Thankin Nu became Burma's first leader after Aung San's death.

room, amid shattered glass and bullet-pocked furniture, Aung San and eight other men lay dead.

Aung San was gone, but the goal he had worked toward for so long—independence for Burma—was finally reached on January 4, 1948. On that day, Burma became an independent nation.

Suu Kyi was just two years old when her father was killed, but she grew up surrounded by evidence of his contributions to Burma. Relatives, friends, and even strangers told stories about him. By simply walking through Rangoon, she was reminded of her father—one of the city's main streets is named Aung San. A market, a park, and a museum also bear his name. A Burmese national holiday, called Martyr's Day, honors his death. From her earliest years, Aung San Suu Kyi learned about duty to her country and devotion to its freedom.

CHAPTER 3

LESSONS FOR LIFE

Women's Equality: A Cultural Heritage

In the 1850s, British officials noted that women in Burma had more rights and greater freedom than women in Europe. There are records of women holding public office in Burma a thousand years ago. Burmese women could own property and voice their opinions on important topics. Suu Kyi witnessed this heritage of equality in the actions of her mother, and she has demonstrated it in her own life.

An early supporter of women's rights speaks to a crowd in England in 1890.

Although the death of her father was a huge loss, Suu Kyi's childhood was full of role models—from within and outside Burma—who helped shape the person she is today.

One of these role models was Suu Kyi's mother, Khin Kyi. After the death of Aung San, Khin Kyi was not content to sit at home. Like her husband, she wanted to serve the people of Burma.

At first, she took Aung San's seat in Burma's new parliament. Khin Kyi was not a politician, however, and she didn't stay in parliament long. Her skills were in nursing and administration, and she was soon appointed chairwoman of the Burmese Council of Social Services.

Suu Kyi's relatives—grandparents, aunts, and uncles—lived nearby, and they gave Khin Kyi plenty of help raising her children. With so many cousins and neighbors, Suu Kyi never had a shortage of other children with whom to play. As a young girl, Suu Kyi liked to play with dolls, but she also was a bit of a tomboy. She played games such as soccer that were usually reserved for boys.

A SECOND TRAGEDY

Suu Kyi's favorite playmate was her brother Aung San Lin. When she was seven, Suu Kyi and Lin were playing near a pond behind their home. As they walked back to their house, Lin realized that he'd lost one of his sandals and ran back to find it.

Aung San Lin drowned in the pond, and Suu Kyi never saw her brother again. It was a terrible loss for the family and especially hard for Suu Kyi. She said later, "I think in some ways the death of my second brother affected me more than my father's death."

LEARNING AND GROWING

Soon after Lin died, Khin Kyi moved her two remaining children to a new home in Rangoon, near Rangoon University. The house was always full. Political and social leaders were frequent guests. Nursing students from all over Burma dropped in and sometimes lived with Suu Kyi's family. From these

Buddhism

More than 85 percent of the Burmese people practice Buddhism. This religious faith began in India about 2,500 years ago and is based on the teachings of Siddartha Gautama, a wealthy prince who gave up his kingdom to search for truth. Living as a beggar, he spread his teachings about how to avoid suffering, and he became known as Buddha, which means "the awakened" or "the enlightened one." (A statue of Buddha is shown above.)

Aung San Suu Kyi has written, "Rulers must observe the teachings of Buddha. Central to these teachings are truth, righteousness, and loving kindness. It is government based on these very qualities that the people of Burma are seeking in their struggle for democracy."

Mahatma Gandhi (1869–1948)

Mohandas Gandhi (below) was a small, frail man who became one of the most famous political figures of the twentieth century. Known as "the Father of India," he almost single-handedly led his country to independence from Great Britain. The Indian people called him *mahatma*, which means "great soul."

Gandhi taught and practiced the ideas of passive resistance and **civil disobedience**. He urged people to disobey unjust laws peacefully and be arrested if necessary but never resort to violence. Gandhi went on hunger strikes, often coming close to death, to persuade people to follow his ideas. His activities landed him in prison many times.

During his life, Gandhi always taught acceptance and tolerance of all people and religions. When India gained independence in 1947, he was heartbroken that the country was divided, according to the dominance of two religions, into two nations: India (Hinduism) and Pakistan (Islam). The following year, he was killed by a religious fanatic.

visitors, Suu Kyi was able to learn the stories and customs of many different ethnic groups.

She especially loved to listen to her great aunt tell stories about Buddha. "She knew the whole story of Buddha's life," Suu Kyi has recalled. "Her knowledge of Buddhism was really very, very broad, and she taught us a lot." Though Suu Kyi was raised as a devout Buddhist, one of her grandfathers was a Christian who taught her to be respectful of all religious faiths.

It was not until Suu Kyi was twelve years old that she overcame her fear of the dark. As she later said, "I could not bear to go into a dark room by myself. I think I was afraid of ghosts, because the Burmese are very fond of ghost stories." Suu Kyi decided to do something about it. She would wait until her mother and brother were asleep, then go downstairs alone and force herself to walk around the house in the dark. After five or six days, she was no longer afraid.

Suu Kyi attended the English Methodist High School, a private school in Rangoon. Instruction was in both Burmese and English, and Suu Kyi became a dedicated reader in both languages. One year, an American named Bob Fuller taught at the school. He was a science teacher, but he also taught a class on **ethics**. Suu Kyi was very impressed by this class. She has said it helped her understand people with different backgrounds and points of view.

A view of Rangoon (now called Yangon) in the 1950s

A NEW LIFE

In 1960, when Suu Kyi was fifteen years old, her mother was appointed Burma's **ambassador** to India. The family moved to the capital of India, New Delhi. In New Delhi, Suu Kyi attended a Catholic high school, where she was taught by Irish nuns. In addition to regular high school subjects, Suu Kyi took piano lessons and learned to ride horses. She also began writing. One year she wrote a humorous version of William Shakespeare's play *Antony and Cleopatra* that was staged by the school's drama club.

Suu Kyi also continued her reading in several languages. Friends of her family sent her books and gave her lists of books she should read. She became especially fond of the writings of Mahatma Gandhi, whose dedication to nonviolence and peaceful civil disobedience helped India gain its independence from Britain.

"A COMMANDING PERSON"

Because her mother was an ambassador, Suu Kyi attended many social events, where she met political figures from India and other countries. A British journalist who visited Suu Kyi's family said, "I remember being struck by how she plunged into conversations about politics. She was seventeen or eighteen, and she was already a commanding person."

After high school, Suu Kyi studied political science for two years at Delhi University. Her remaining brother, Aung San U, had already finished high school and was studying engineering in England. Suu Kyi decided to follow him. She applied to, and was accepted by, England's world-famous Oxford University, where she was to study political science and economics.

Reading has been a lifelong passion for Daw Suu Kyi.

When Suu Kyi arrived in England in 1964, she found a place that was very different from Burma or India. The food, the weather, and the culture were all new to her, and it was quite a while before she began to feel comfortable.

BLUE JEANS AND ROMANCE

At the time, blue jeans and short skirts were the usual dress for young people, but Suu Kyi continued to wear the traditional Burmese ankle-length skirt, called a *longyi*. It would be two years before she put on a pair of jeans—and then only so she could ride a bicycle.

Students gather to talk on the campus of Oxford University.

While some of her classmates at Oxford attended all-night parties and drank heavily, Suu Kyi studied long hours and did not drink. She did try alcohol once, when she and two friends drank a small bottle of liquor one night in the ladies' room of the university library. Suu Kyi hated it, and she never drank again.

Some friends of Suu Kyi's family helped her adjust to life in England. Paul Gore-Booth had been the British ambassador to Burma and had later worked in India. He and his wife Patricia invited Suu Kyi

The Old Man

General Ne Win (above) fought with Suu Kyi's father against the Japanese during World War II and became commander in chief of the army after the war. In 1962, he seized control of Burma's government. Over the next twenty-six years, Ne Win created one of the cruelest, most **repressive** governments in Asia. People in Burma were afraid to speak his name, and they usually referred to him as "number one" or "the old man." In 2002, Ne Win was arrested for plotting to overthrow the government he helped create. He remained a prisoner in his own home until his death that same year.

to stay with them on holidays and school breaks. One of the people she met at their home was a curly-haired young Englishman named Michael Aris, who was studying the history, customs, and languages of Asia. Mrs. Gore-Booth later said that Michael fell in love with Suu Kyi immediately. Although Michael attended school in London, about 60 miles (97 kilometers) from Oxford, the two saw each other relatively often. After college, however, they pursued separate lives that put considerable distance between them.

TROUBLE IN BURMA

By the time Suu Kyi began college, life in Burma had changed dramatically. In March 1962, an army general named Ne Win had led a military takeover of the country. He ordered Burma's parliament shut down and arrested the country's elected leaders, including Prime Minister U Nu.

Ne Win quickly formed a new political party made up almost entirely of military officers. People who protested the new government were attacked by soldiers or arrested. Ne Win forced all U.S. and European citizens to leave the country. The military took over all banks, schools, and communication systems, as well as many of the country's businesses.

Suu Kyi's mother disapproved of Ne Win's government, but she believed that she could best serve the people of Burma by remaining an ambassador to her country. Conditions in Burma, however, became progressively worse. Ne Win's soldiers knew little about running Burma's institutions and businesses, and eventually there were severe shortages of food, fuel, and other materials throughout the country.

MOVING TO AMERICA

Suu Kyi graduated from Oxford in 1968. Soon after graduating, she left England for New York City. She lived with a family friend, an older Burmese woman named Daw Than E, who worked for the United Nations (UN). Suu Kyi intended to study at New York University, but Daw Than E encouraged her to apply for work at the UN. Suu Kyi was hired, and she

Martin Luther King Jr. (1929–1968)

Burma was not the only nation in turmoil during the 1960s. The decade was a troubled time in the United States as well. The civil rights movement was at its peak, and Dr. Martin Luther King Jr. (below) was one of the movement's leaders. He believed deeply in Mahatma Gandhi's principles of nonviolence and civil disobedience, and he applied those principles to help African-Americans in their drive for equal rights. Like Gandhi, King was arrested many times but continued to practice peaceful resistance to unjust laws. King won the Nobel Peace Prize in 1964. He was shot and killed in Memphis, Tennessee, in 1968.

Aung San Suu Kyi followed the news of Dr. King and the civil rights movement while she was a student in England. She later said, "I have been moved by Martin Luther King's 'I Have A Dream' speech, and how he tried to better the lot of black people without fostering feelings of hate."

The United Nations (UN) headquarters in New York City

eventually worked on a committee that kept track of the finances for all UN departments and programs.

In the United States, Suu Kyi continued to seek new challenges. While living in New York, for example, she did volunteer work at Bellevue Hospital, a facility that cared for some of the poorest and neediest people in the city. She also visited Boston and Washington, D.C., and she once rode a bus all the way to California.

NEWS FROM BURMA

When Suu Kyi was working at the UN, the UN Secretary General was a Burmese man named U Thant. Attending parties at U Thant's New York home, Suu Kyi celebrated Burmese holidays and enjoyed Burmese food. She also spent time with the Burmese **delegates** to the UN.

Speaking "off the record," the delegates would give Suu Kyi news about what was really happening in Burma, and she was able to talk freely with them. At official functions, however, the delegates did not dare criticize the Burmese government, because Ne Win's representatives were among them.

FALLING IN LOVE

While Suu Kyi was in New York City, Michael Aris was 10,000 miles away in the tiny, mountainous kingdom of

Bhutan. After graduating from Durham University in London, he had taken a job as a **tutor** to the royal family of Bhutan. He continued his study of Asian languages and culture, and he wrote a lot of letters to Suu Kyi.

Suu Kyi was worried. She felt she was falling in love with Michael Aris, and she didn't know how her family and friends at home would feel about it. Many people in Burma believed that Burmese who married foreigners were rejecting their culture and heritage. Suu Kyi didn't want anyone to have such a belief about her.

"I ASK ONLY ONE THING"

Late in 1970, Suu Kyi returned to Burma to visit her mother, who had retired as an ambassador. On the way back to New York, she stopped in Bhutan to visit Michael. By the time she got back on the plane, she and Michael were engaged to be married. All through 1971, the two wrote letters to each other—187 letters in all. In one letter, Suu Kyi wrote, "I ask only one thing, that should my people need me, you would help me to do my duty to them. Sometimes

Happy newlyweds: Suu Kyi and Michael in the early 1970s

I am beset by fears that circumstances might tear us apart just when we are so happy."

Suu Kyi and Michael were married on New Year's Day, 1972, in a Buddhist ceremony at the Gore-Booth home in London. They returned to Bhutan, where Michael continued working for the royal family. With her UN experience, Suu Kyi was able to get a job with Bhutan's Foreign Ministry as an adviser on United Nations policies.

THE GLOBE-TROTTING FAMILY

In 1973, the young couple returned to England. They found a tiny apartment in London, and Michael began to write and study for his **doctorate degree**. Suu Kyi learned to sew and to cook English, French, and Burmese food. The couple's first child, whom they named Alexander, was born in April of 1973. In 1976, Michael received a fellowship from Oxford University, and the family moved to Oxford. In September, 1977, the couple's second son was born. They named him Kim.

Michael Aris with his sons Kim (center) and Alexander in London in 1991

While caring for her sons, Suu Kyi wrote a biography of her father. Titled simply *Aung San*, the book was published in 1984. While writing it, she became interested in her father's activities in Japan during World War II. Suu Kyi taught herself to speak Japanese. She then spent a year in Japan while she completed her research. Kim lived with her, while Alex lived with Michael in India, where he had received a scholarship to study. Suu Kyi and Kim joined Michael and Alex in 1986.

In 1987, the whole family finally returned to England. The boys continued school. They were growing up being exposed to books and foreign languages, and they met visitors from many different cultures. Alex enjoyed sports and philosophy, while Kim read and played the guitar. Michael continued his research and writing.

A LIFE-CHANGING CALL

Suu Kyi had always made sure to keep the culture and history of Burma alive in her home. Her sons, for example, were taught to read and speak Burmese, and they were instructed in the Buddhist religion. The family also followed many Burmese customs. Once back in England, Suu Kyi wrote a short book called *Let's Visit Burma*. She also planned to study Burmese literature at London University.

Suu Kyi's involvement with Burma, however, would soon increase dramatically. In March 1988, she received a late-night phone call from Burma and learned that her mother, Khin Kyi, had suffered a severe stroke and was in a hospital in Rangoon. Suu Kyi immediately flew to Burma so she could be by her mother's side.

CHAPTER 5

A DUTY TO GET INVOLVED

Suu Kyi's life in England was quite different from the lives of most people in Burma. Since the military takeover in 1962, conditions in the country had become steadily worse.

THE PEOPLE'S OUTRAGE

Burma had been a prosperous nation, and at one time it had provided one-third of the world's total supply of rice. By 1988, however, after twenty-six years of Ne Win's military government, Burma had to import rice from other countries. Health care, education, transportation, and communication services—even something as basic as a telephone—were available only to the wealthy, and the only wealthy people in Burma were those with connections to the government. Yet despite the government's obvious failings, no one was allowed to criticize it or protest against its policies. Those who did were imprisoned or simply disappeared.

On the night of March 12, 1988, in a teahouse in Rangoon, a fight broke out between a group of students and some local men. During the brawl, a

During a demonstration in Rangoon in 1988, anti-government marchers carry pictures of Suu Kyi's father, Aung San, to show their support for democracy.

student was stabbed. The local men were arrested, but when it was discovered that one of the men was the son of a government official, they were all set free. Students and other citizens were outraged, and they took to the streets in protest. The government responded with riot police and soldiers. Hundreds of people were killed, and hundreds more were beaten and dragged off to prison.

Suu Kyi stepped into this situation when she arrived at Rangoon hospital to see her mother. For the next three months, she stayed by her mother's bedside. Outside the hospital, meanwhile, the struggle for Burma's future continued.

STRIKES AND DEMONSTRATIONS

Throughout June and July of 1988, students staged demonstrations in cities across Burma. They were joined by factory workers who went on strike to show support for them. Ne Win's army and police continued to beat and arrest the protestors, who began to use home-made weapons to fight back. Suu Kyi could see some of these demonstrations from the hospital window. She worried, because she knew that violence would only bring further violence. She believed that only peaceful dialogue with the government would bring change.

The violence increased. In an effort to calm the population, Ne Win called for a **referendum** on democratic reforms. He also announced his retirement. But everyone believed that, retired or not, Ne Win would still be running the country.

During this time, it became clear that Daw Khin Kyi would not recover. Suu Kyi moved her mother from the hospital to her home on University Avenue, where she would be surrounded by friends and family. Among the people who came to pay their

respects were U Tin U, a former general who had been imprisoned by Ne Win, and U Nu, the prime minister whom Ne Win had overthrown. These men urged Suu Kyi to become part of the democracy movement.

AN AWFUL MASSACRE

A Burmese student protester in 1988. The bird on his headband symbolizes opposition to the military government.

Armed soldiers patrol the streets of Rangoon in August 1988.

Students were no longer the only Burmese people who were demonstrating against the government. They had been joined by businessmen, farmers, lawyers, dock workers, housewives, Buddhist monks, doctors, and bus drivers. Demonstration leaders decided to stage a nationwide strike on August 8th. The strikers thought the repetition of numbers in the date—8/8/88—would bring them good luck. They were very wrong.

On the morning of August 8, in what became known as the "Four Eights" strike, a hundred thousand people in Rangoon walked off their jobs and took to the streets. Thousands more watched and cheered them on. Some of the strikers simply sat in the streets. Many more marched. Even a few soldiers joined them. They gathered in front of City Hall, in parks, and near the hospital. The people listened to speeches against the military government and its policies.

The demonstrations were peaceful and lasted all day and into the night. Just before midnight, however, trucks full of armed soldiers surrounded the crowd at City Hall. When the people saw the soldiers, they began singing the Burmese national anthem. The soldiers responded with machine gun fire, and people died by the dozens. The crowd ran in all directions, but the soldiers kept firing. At Rangoon hospital, doctors and nurses who came outside to treat the wounded were themselves shot. Throughout the city, the sound of gunfire continued until morning.

Strikers and other demonstrators were attacked in every city in the country. No one knows how many were killed, but from witness accounts, as many as ten thousand unarmed people may have died.

The Shwe Dagon Pagoda

The Shwe Dagon Pagoda (below) is the most famous and most photographed place in Myanmar. It is a walled complex containing more than a hundred temples, shrines, and other buildings, and it has been growing in size on the same site for almost a thousand years. Inside the main pagoda is a small shrine containing eight hairs said to be from Buddha's head. The dome on the main pagoda is over 300 feet (90 meters) high and is covered with gold. Shwe Dagon is a center of Buddhist learning and is home to many monks and religious scholars.

THE LADY SPEAKS

Suu Kyi sits with U Nu (left) and U Tin U (right) at one of the first meetings of the National League for Democracy (NLD).

Once again, Suu Kyi was approached by former general U Tin U and her father's old friend U Nu. They wanted to form a political party, and they asked her to join. They thought that having Aung San's daughter among them would make the new party more appealing.

The violence of the Four Eights strike convinced Suu Kyi that she had to do something for her country. She said, "This is not a time for anyone who cares to stay out. As my father's daughter, I felt I had a duty to get involved." She announced that she would give a speech at the Shwe Dagon Pagoda, a Rangoon landmark.

People began gathering at the pagoda twenty-four hours before the speech. By the time Suu Kyi arrived, a crowd of people estimated at a half million had assembled, all wanting to hear what Aung San's daughter had to say. She called for the Burmese people to make democracy their goal and demanded that the military government abandon the one-party political system and hold free elections. With this speech, Suu Kyi placed herself in direct opposition to the military government.

THE SLORC VS. THE NLD

Within days, a general named Saw Maung took control of the government. Saw Maung announced that the new government would be called the State Law and Order

"These Are Our Demands"

Suu Kyi began her speech at the Shwe Dagon Pagoda by asking the half-million people present to remain calm and observe a moment of silence for those who had been killed in the previous weeks. She knew some people were concerned because she had lived abroad and had married a foreigner. She said, "These facts will never interfere with or lessen my love and devotion for my country."

Her father's tomb is near the Shwe Dagon Pagoda, and Suu Kyi read aloud some words Aung San had written: "We must make democracy the popular creed. Democracy is the only **ideology** which is consistent with freedom. It is also the only ideology that promotes and strengthens peace. Therefore, it is the only ideology we should aim for."

Suu Kyi said, "The present crisis is the concern of the entire nation. I could not, as my father's daughter, remain indifferent to all that was going on. This national crisis could, in fact, be called the second struggle for national independence." Finally, speaking directly to the military government, she said, "The one-party system should be dismantled, [and] a multi-party system of government should be established. We call for free and fair elections to be arranged as quickly as possible. These are our demands."

Restoration Council (SLORC). Although Saw Maung did not want the democracy movement to succeed, he promised that one-party rule would end and that Burma would hold national elections.

A few days later, the democracy movement formed its own political party, the National League for Democracy (NLD). Suu Kyi was made secretary general. The party leaders began to travel all over Burma, working to gain support from all ethnic and minority groups. Suu Kyi often wore ethnic clothing and had her speeches translated into minority languages. People admired her, and large crowds gathered everywhere she went.

In December 1988, Suu Kyi's mother died. More than a hundred thousand people attended her funeral. Soon after, Suu Kyi resumed traveling and speaking.

In July, 1989, the SLORC announced that national elections would be held in the spring of 1990. The NLD stepped up its campaign activities, and the SLORC increased its efforts to disrupt them. When meetings were held in buildings, soldiers put barricades on the roads nearby and arrested anyone crossing them. At outdoor meetings, army trucks would blast music from loudspeakers, drowning out the speakers' voices. Suu Kyi planned a march to her father's tomb on the anniversary of his assassination. The SLORC placed thousands of soldiers along the roads and threatened to shoot anyone who marched there. Suu Kyi canceled the event to avoid a massacre.

The NLD was becoming a real threat to the military government, and the SLORC was determined to eliminate it. On the morning of July 20, 1989, U Tin U and U Nu were arrested and taken to prison. Soldiers surrounded Suu Kyi's home and placed her under house arrest. She was not permitted to leave her home, and no one was allowed in without permission from the SLORC. Suu Kyi—"The Lady"—would remain in this personal prison for nearly six years.

Suu Kyi speaks at an NLD campaign rally in 1989. Soon after this photo was taken, she was placed under house arrest.

A PRIZE WITHOUT PEACE

By arresting the NLD leaders, the SLORC thought it had killed the democracy movement. They underestimated Aung San Suu Kyi and the Burmese people.

HUNGER STRIKE

Fearing that the other NLD leaders might be tortured or killed, Suu Kyi demanded to be sent to the same prison. The SLORC refused, so Suu Kyi adopted the nonviolent tactics of Mahatma Ghandi and began a hunger strike. She refused to eat until the government guaranteed the proper treatment of her friends. Newspapers and magazines around the world printed the story of her hunger strike. After ten days, the SLORC gave in to her demands.

Suu Kyi stands in front of her family home on University Avenue in Yangon (Rangoon) in 1995.

Suu Kyi's sons, Alex and Kim, were with her when she was arrested. Michael Aris was in England, but he quickly traveled to join her. Suu Kyi's health suffered from the hunger strike, and her husband and sons stayed with her while she recovered. In early September, the boys had to return to England for the start of the school year. Michael went with them. It would be years before the family was together again.

Barbed wire and barricades went up all around Suu Kyi's house. She was cut off from her family and friends, but her sense of duty and self-discipline kept her going. She established a daily routine that included listening to radio news broadcasts from England and the United States, exercise, reading, and meditation. Friends sent her food, books, and money, but the SLORC decided what she actually received. During her years under arrest, she was forced to sell much of her furniture to buy food.

In England, Michael Aris remembered the promise he'd made to his wife years before: that should Suu Kyi's people need her, he would help her to fulfill her duty to them. Aris did all he could. He collected some of Suu Kyi's speeches, letters, and other writings and put

Nelson Mandela speaks to reporters in 2003. He is standing in front of the prison cell in which he was held for twenty-seven years.

Nelson Mandela: Hope For Change

The struggle of Nelson Mandela was one of the news stories Suu Kyi followed though radio broadcasts. Mandela was a leader of the movement to end **apartheid** in South Africa. In that country, Africans (and Asians) had been completely dominated by a white minority for decades, but they were at last gaining equality. Mandela used Gandhi's ideas of nonviolence and passive resistance to change the South African government's policies, but he spent twenty-seven years in prison for his efforts. In 1993, he won the Nobel Peace Prize, and in 1994, he became the first black president of South Africa. Suu Kyi read Mandela's book, *No Easy Walk to Freedom*, while under house arrest. Mandela's success in changing South Africa gave Suu Kyi hope for change in her own country.

them together as a book titled *Freedom From Fear*. Profits from the book were used to buy Suu Kyi food and other necessities.

A CLEAR VICTORY

With the NLD leaders under arrest, the SLORC was no longer worried about holding elections. The SLORC was so confident of winning that it invited foreign journalists into the country to observe the elections. The government wanted to show the world that the voting was free and fair.

These journalists did confirm that the elections of May 1990 were free and fair. The results, however, were not what the SLORC expected. In every part of the country, people voted for the NLD in overwhelming numbers. Suu Kyi's party won 80 percent of the seats in Burma's new legislature.

It was a great victory, but the SLORC would not tolerate this challenge to its power. The SLORC immediately declared that the elections had only been held to choose representatives to write a new **constitution** and *not* to elect a new government. Since the newly-elected representatives were not allowed to meet, however, a new constitution could not be written. The SLORC rapidly and violently clamped down on anyone who protested.

NLD supporters stand in front of posters of Suu Kyi and U Tin U on election day, May 27, 1990.

In October 1991, Aung San Suu Kyi was named the winner of that year's Nobel Peace Prize. She was the first person ever to receive the prize while under arrest. The SLORC would not let her leave Burma (now called Myanmar), so at the awards ceremony in December, her son Alex read the acceptance speech she had written.

In the speech, Suu Kyi stated, "When I wrote to the Nobel Committee, I did say that I was very grateful that they had recognized our cause. I think of all my colleagues who have suffered much more, but who have not been recognized. My recognition really stems from the courage and suffering of many, many others."

Suu Kyi had the money from the prize—one million dollars—put into a fund for the health and education of the Burmese people.

The worldwide recognition of Daw Suu Kyi and her efforts was a major embarrassment to the SLORC. In response, it further tightened its grip on the Burmese people.

Alfred Nobel

Alfred Nobel and the Nobel Prizes

Alfred Nobel (1863–1896), for whom the Nobel Prize is named, was a Swedish scientist and inventor. In 1863, he developed an explosive called nitroglycerine, and in 1867 he invented a special type of nitroglycerine that he called "dynamite". Nobel's invention quickly made him one of the richest men in Europe. When Nobel died, he left most of his wealth to a fund. He specified that the interest the money in the fund earned each year was to be given to people whose work had benefited mankind. Every December, the Nobel Committee awards prizes for work in chemistry, physics, medicine, literature, and world peace.

REPRESSION AND DRUGS

Many Burmese ethnic groups had armed themselves and were fighting government soldiers in the hills and jungles. The SLORC created a special policy to control them. Whole provinces were declared military zones, and the ethnic people there were forced to live in fenced compounds. In other parts of the country, hundreds of thousands of people were forced into slave labor, either for construction projects or for the army. The SLORC called this forced labor the "people's contributions" to the government.

Before they escaped, these men were forced to work as slave laborers for the SLORC's army.

In the border areas near Thailand and Laos, SLORC soldiers took control of poppy fields. Poppy flowers are the source of opium, from which heroin and other illegal drugs are made. The sale of these drugs became a major source of income for the military government.

RELEASE AT LAST

By 1994, the SLORC was trying very hard to get loans from foreign banks and private investors. To make a better impression on the outside world—particularly the United States—the government decided to ease some of its restrictions on its famous prisoner.

Suu Kyi was permitted a visit from U.S. Congressman Bill Richardson. It was the first time in over five years that she'd been allowed to meet anyone outside of her own family. Richardson reported that Daw Suu Kyi's first concern was democracy for her country. She also missed her family and had some health

The Story of Myin

American journalist Mark Jenkins wrote of visiting a Buddhist monastery in India, near the Burmese border. There he met a boy named Myin who is a Kachin, one of the ethnic minority groups in northern Myanmar. Some Kachins have been fighting a guerrilla war against the military government for many years. In 1994, government soldiers came to Myin's village, burned it to the ground, and took all of the young boys. The soldiers were tracking pro-democracy rebels in the jungles. They knew the trails were booby-trapped, so they forced Myin and the other boys to walk in front of them. Myin was seven years old when he stepped on a land mine. His left leg was blown off at the hip. When Suu Kyi and others speak of "human rights abuses" by the Burmese government, they are talking about Myin and tens of thousands of people like him.

Suu Kyi speaks to her supporters at the main gate of her home in Yangon in 1995.

problems. Congressman Richardson offered to get her medical care and better food, but Suu Kyi refused. She told him that the SLORC had offered those things too. She didn't want anyone—especially members of the SLORC—to think that her cooperation could be purchased with comforts and conveniences.

On June 19, 1995, Suu Kyi's fiftieth birthday, human rights groups around the world demonstrated for her freedom and against the SLORC's policies. On July 10, the military government suddenly announced that The Lady was free.

Michael, Alex, and Kim traveled to Rangoon (now officially called Yangon). They had a joyful, though brief, reunion with Suu Kyi. Once again, the boys and their father had to return to England for the beginning of the school year. No one knew that it was the last time the family would all be together.

If Myanmar's military leaders thought six years of house arrest had made Daw Suu Kyi less willing to criticize them, they were wrong. Her message remained the same: Nonviolence is the only way to bring about effective change. Democracy is the goal. The SLORC must hold free elections.

THE PEOPLE WANT DEMOCRACY

Suu Kyi began holding Sunday afternoon meetings at her home. Despite the soldiers and barricades brought in to discourage them, hundreds, sometimes thousands, of people would gather on the street outside her house. They asked questions and listened to what The Lady had to say about Myanmar's condition and future.

She told them, "It's very simple. You must not forget that the people of Burma want democracy. Whatever the authorities may say, it is a fact that the people want democracy and they do not want an **authoritarian** regime that deprives them of their basic human rights."

Supporters cheer during one of Suu Kyi's weekly speeches. Her home is surrounded by barbed wire and barricades.

In the years following her release, Suu Kyi and the other NLD leaders played a dangerous game of action and reaction. If Suu Kyi attracted a large crowd, soldiers used fire hoses and barricades to break it up. When the NLD planned a meeting, the SLORC arrested people before they could attend. Every time Suu Kyi tried to travel outside of Yangon, she ran into roadblocks. When Michael, Alex, and Kim tried to visit her, the SLORC refused to let them enter Myanmar. Suu Kyi said, "Nothing has changed since my release. Let the world know that we are still prisoners within our own country."

The Yadana Pipeline

The Yadana pipeline is the largest foreign investment project in Myanmar. Designed to carry natural gas from Myanmar's off-shore wells across the country and into Thailand, it is being built by a French and a U.S. company. In March, 2003, the U.S. company, Unocal, was brought to trial in Los Angeles for its involvement in human rights violations. Unocal was being charged with ignoring the Burmese government's use of forced labor and the forced relocation of Burmese citizens in the construction of the Yadana pipeline.

BOYCOTT

In 1997, the SLORC changed its name to the State Peace and Development Council (SPDC). Myanmar's military leaders thought the new name would sound better to outsiders. They were still trying very hard to attract foreign investors, as well as tourists.

Suu Kyi urged foreign companies not to invest money in Myanmar. She pointed out that the government used forced labor for many of the projects paid for with those investments. She said that profits went to a few military leaders, not to the Burmese people. For the same reasons, she asked tourists to **boycott** Myanmar. In response, the SPDC stepped up harassment of Suu Kyi and the NLD. Suu Kyi had endured such harassment before. But for her, matters were about to get much worse.

In 1998, Michael Aris was diagnosed with cancer. He applied for visas so he and the boys could visit Myanmar. The SPDC refused to allow Aris into the country, then publicly encouraged Suu Kyi to go to England to be with her family. She was in a horrible position. She desperately wanted to be with her husband and sons but was certain that if she left, she would never be allowed to reenter Myanmar. Suu Kyi stayed in Yangon.

On March 27, 1999, his fifty-third birthday, Michael Aris died in England. His sons Alex and Kim were with him. Half a world away, Aung San Suu Kyi wept alone.

Michael Aris

Alex Aris (left) accepts the Medal of Freedom for his mother from U.S. president Bill Clinton (right).

"Fearful Weapons"

The Presidential Medal of Freedom is the highest award given to civilians by the United States government. In December 2000, U.S. president Bill Clinton awarded the medal to Suu

Kyi. Her son Alex accepted it for her in Washington, D.C. President Clinton said, "The defenders of human rights need our support in Burma. Their only weapons are words, reason, and the brave example of Aung San Suu Kyi. But these are fearful weapons to the ruling regime."

A young supporter holds a poster demanding Suu Kyi's release from house arrest.

ARRESTED AGAIN

Suu Kyi put aside her sadness and returned to the struggle for democracy. In August 2000, she and a number of companions were traveling by car to organize NLD workers. Soldiers blocked the road and ordered them to turn around. Suu Kyi refused, and for nine days her group stayed on the road with little food or water. The standoff ended when two hundred riot police forced Suu Kyi back to Yangon. She was then placed under house arrest again.

For the next two years, the United States, the United Nations, and the European Union all sent representatives to Burma. They met with both members of the SPDC and Suu Kyi, trying to begin a dialogue between them about Myanmar's future. The SPDC's generals eventually met with Suu Kyi and other NLD leaders, and on May 6, 2002, she was released from house arrest. The SPDC, however, still refused to write a constitution, allow free elections, or tolerate any opposition.

MORE VIOLENCE

In April 2003, Suu Kyi strongly criticized the government for refusing to begin meaningful political talks

"She Is a Giant"

Archbishop Desmond Tutu (left) is a friend and colleague of Nelson Mandela. Archbishop Tutu won the 1984 Nobel Peace Prize for his work in the anti-apartheid movement in South Africa. In 2001, on the tenth anniversary of Suu Kyi's Nobel Prize, Tutu said, "In physical stature she is petite and elegant, but in **moral** stature she is a giant. Big men are afraid of her. Armed to the teeth, and they still run scared."

with her. Across Myanmar, more and more people began attending meetings where The Lady spoke. The military government became more determined to stop her.

Suu Kyi had been lucky. In the years since her return to Burma, her father's position as the country's greatest hero had protected her. Other democracy supporters had been imprisoned, tortured, or killed, but the government was more cautious with the daughter of Aung San. This luck was about to run out.

On May 30, 2003, an incident occurred that is still wrapped in contradictions and secrecy. Suu Kyi and a number of her supporters were traveling in a convoy of cars in northern Myanmar. They came to a military roadblock, and gunfire broke out. At least four people were killed, and as many as fifty were injured.

Some said it was an assassination attempt. The SPDC claimed that the soldiers and riot police were provoked. Suu Kyi was arrested and taken to prison. For months, no one was allowed to see her or speak to her.

The government called her imprisonment "protective custody." In September, she was transferred to a hospital for surgery. When she recovered, she was once again placed under house arrest.

FREEDOM FROM FEAR

At the time of this writing, Aung San Suu Kyi is still confined to her home in Yangon. She is cut off from her sons, her supporters, and the outside world. But though she is isolated, she is not alone. Human rights groups and other concerned people around the world are speaking out on her behalf. When visiting Thailand in October 2003, U.S. president George Bush said, "We care deeply about Aung San Suu Kyi and her status, and we would like to see her free."

Like her homeland, Aung San Suu Kyi is still waiting to be free.

Aung San Suu Kyi wants Myanmar to be free—of oppression, violence, lies, and fear. In an interview, she once said, "I think most people are afraid of loss. They're afraid of losing their friends, their liberty, their means of livelihood. Basically they're afraid of losing what they have or losing the opportunity to live decent lives. What people want is freedom from that kind of fear."

In a crumbling, water-stained old house in Yangon, The Lady is still leading the struggle for a country that is waiting to be free.

A Free Bird

A poem by Aung San Suu Kyi

My home...
where I was born and raised
used to be warm and lively
now filled with darkness and horror

My family...
whom I had grown with
used to be cheerful and lively
now living with fear and terror

My friends...
whom I shared my life with
used to be pure and merry
now living with wounded hearts

A free bird...
which is just freed
used to be caged
now flying with an olive branch
for the place it loves

A free bird towards a free Burma

TIMELINE

1945	Aung San Suu Kyi is born on June 19
1947	Suu Kyi's father, Aung San, is assassinated on July 19
1960	Suu Kyi's mother, Khin Kyi, is appointed Burma's ambassador to India
1962	Ne Win becomes military dictator of Burma
1964	Suu Kyi begins attending Oxford University in England
1968	Completes her degree in political science and economics
1969	Moves to New York and begins working at the United Nations
1972	Marries Michael Aris; moves to Bhutan
1973	Moves to London; her first son, Alexander Aris, is born
1977	Kim Aris, Suu Kyi's second son, is born
1984	Suu Kyi publishes a biography of her father, Aung San
1988	Returns to Burma after her mother, Khin Kyi, suffers a stroke; The Four Eights protests take place, and thousands of Burmese citizens are killed; Suu Kyi delivers her first major speech; the National League for Democracy (NLD) is formed, and Suu Kyi is appointed general secretary; Suu Kyi's mother dies
1989	The military government changes the name of Burma to Myanmar; Suu Kyi is placed under house arrest and other NLD leaders are imprisoned
1990	NLD wins landslide victory in elections but is not allowed to form a civilian government
1991	Suu Kyi wins the Nobel Peace Prize
1995	Released from house arrest
1999	Michael Aris dies of cancer
2000	After a roadblock incident, Suu Kyi is placed under house arrest again; receives the Medal of Freedom from the U.S. government
2002	Released from house arrest
2003	Injured in a roadblock incident and sent to prison; after several months, is returned to house arrest

ambassador: the official representative for a country in another country.

apartheid: a system of laws and practices once used in South Africa to separate people by race.

authoritarian: having to do with a small group holding all power in a country and oppressing the country's citizens.

boycott: refusing to buy a product, use a service, or take part in an activity as a form of protest.

civil disobedience: the act of disobeying certain laws, usually as a protest.

constitution: a set of laws that establish how a country is governed.

delegates: people who represent others at a conference or in an organization.

dictatorship: a government in which one person or a very small group of people holds absolute power.

doctorate degree: the highest degree a university can give to a person

ethics: the study or discussion of what is considered right and wrong.

ethnic: related to a particular race, religion, culture, or region.

human rights: freedoms and protections that all people should have.

ideology: a system of beliefs and ideas.

malaria: a disease carried by mosquitos that results in chills and fevers.

moral: related to right and wrong ways of behaving.

oppression: unjust or brutal use of power, such as by a dictatorship.

parliamentary: related to a parliament, which is a body of representatives elected to make a country's laws.

referendum: a popular vote to decide on a particular proposal.

repressive: related to actions that deny people their rights.

transitional: related to the process of changing from one organization or way of doing things to another.

tutor: a person who provides individual instruction, usually in a private setting.

TO FIND OUT MORE

BOOKS

Aung San Suu Kyi. **Freedom From Fear**. New York: Penguin, 1996.

Aung San Suu Kyi. **Letters from Burma**. New York: Penguin, 1998.

Aung San Suu Kyi and Alan Clements. **The Voice of Hope**. New York: Seven Stories Press, 1998.

Hacker, Carlotta. **Nobel Prize Winners (Women in Profile)**. New York: Crabtree Publishing, 1998.

Khng, Pauline. **Myanmar (Countries of the World)**. Milwaukee: Gareth Stevens, 2000.

Ling, Bettina and Charlotte Bunch. **Aung San Suu Kyi: Standing Up for Democracy in Burma (Women Changing the World)**. New York: The Feminist Press at CUNY, 1999

Stewart, Whitney. **Aung San Suu Kyi: Fearless Voice of Burma**. Minneapolis: Lerner Publications, 1997.

INTERNET SITES

Burma Project
www.burmaproject.org
Features information about health and human rights issues in Burma, plus news, maps, and a special section on the history and people of the 1988 strikes and demonstrations.

Burmanet News
www.burmanet.org
A collection of articles about recent events in Burma from newspapers and radio stations around the world.

Daw Aung San Suu Kyi
www.dassk.org
Includes pictures, current news, speeches, interviews, sounds and videos, letters to Daw Suu Kyi, awards, press releases, and more.

Nobel e-Museum: The Nobel Peace Prize Laureates
www.nobel.se/peace/laureates
Information about all of the people who have won the Nobel Peace Prize, including Aung San Suu Kyi.

About the Author

William Thomas is a school teacher who lives in Rochester, New York. A former Peace Corps Volunteer, he holds graduate degrees from Rochester Institute of Technology and Nazareth College. When not teaching or writing, Bill enjoys time with his family, playing his guitar, canoeing, and backpacking. He claims he was once King of Fiji but gave up the throne to pursue a career as a relief pitcher. It's not true.